# MY 6 MOTHERS

DR. NAVDEEP

ISBN 979-888546328-7

# Contents

# I
# INTRODUCTION

At the very outset, I extend my deepest gratitude and warm regards to all the mothers out there for their multifaceted personalities and obligations that they successfully carry out without an iota of exhaustion, the major one being obediently playing their role. This true outpour of my heart is actually to showcase the role of numerous women, people, organisations and institutions that I have come across in the journey of life, the collective teachings, preachings and the blessings of whom have added up in making me a near-perfect individual. I am indeed fortunate and privileged to grow under the wings of my 6 Mothers.

I do understand and respect my biological mother, but I don't give full credit to her in what I am today because of the very many innumerable environmental factors which have finally cast me into a good doctor and perhaps into a good human being.. I know I may be wrong in my thinking that led me to write all this as this is quite contrary to the usual belief of giving full marks to our mothers as a whole in making any individual's personality. I fully and consciously apologise for any hurt inflicted on my biological. I love her and have a deep unconditional respect for her and would continue praying to the unknown power to bless me with her in all my incarnations.

I also very well understand the joys of raising children for any woman, and I fully acknowledge the pains through which my biological mother must have gone in delivering me and caring for me so very softly and carefully during my whole childhood period. I don't underestimate her feelings, affections, love, generosity and the way she empowered me. She lived, lives and would continue to live in my soul in time to come.

I am not biased towards any of my mothers but simply feel very lucky and proud to be a product of the combined efforts of all 6. Their efforts, love, and concerns, combined with pure dedication, commitment, and passion, led to my artistic crafting to produce a masterpiece called Navdeep. May God bless them all always, and I will continue to pray for all of them to be with me in my reincarnations.

# II
# My First Mother...

## MY BIOLOGICAL MOTHER
## MRS NARINDER PAUL KAUR

My first Mother is my biological mother, who gave birth to me on Sunday, 11th August 1969 at around 9.45 PM in our ancestral home in Amritsar. As all mothers are, she definitely would have been extremely happy on my arrival. I don't recollect any of my early childhood memories, but the first memorable event of hers with me, which I very clearly remember, is of being joyous and happy. She would very frequently carry me on her back and give me lots and lots of swings. I used to burst into loads of laughter. This must have made her joyous and satisfied. The very emotional bond of love I share with her is so deeply engraved in my heart that it can hardly be erased.

Life moved on; I started growing. As time passed, she blessed me with more and more love, profound warmth, eternal happiness, affection, and pampering. Life was as if I was born with a silver spoon, ample to eat, ample to enjoy, ample to laugh; I never experienced sadness.

Perhaps never knew what bad times are. She bought me up in a kingly fashion. She would make sure that I eat fresh food, drink well, sleep well, play well, study well, and enjoy and laugh well.

I was very, very fond of watching films, especially Amitabh Bachchan's movies during my childhood. We both would very eagerly scan every Friday's newspaper to find out new weekly releases and then would hire a rickshaw even during scorching summers to reach the theatre early so as not to miss even a second of the Film. She always accompanied me to watch films, would buy me a chilled coke, popcorns and at times five star Cadbury chocolate in the interval. Such an understanding and considerate mother is like God's gift. She would very easily read my heart and adjust her own schedule to fulfil my desires. Psychological perfection and emotional intelligence were her strongest assets. I don't deny or defy the fact that all mothers are not understanding, but I am simply showcasing her qualities that I try to carry forward in my life and transform myself as an ideal parent to my kids just like my mother was to me.

She loved eggs and used to make "egg bhurji," which was available all day. Tomato fish was another dish which she was good at. Serving "Allo ke paranthe" on some Sunday's was her routine whenever any relative used to visit us. Her kitchen was always full of mangoes, biscuits, and almonds. She loved dry fruits. Her custom of keeping a dozen or so of dry almonds soaked in a cup of water overnight to enjoy the next day is still being followed very religiously and meticulously every night to date.

Genes don't lie. I am a perfect blend of genetic perfection with environmental influence shaping me into the person I am today. I thank her for giving me half the set of her wonderful chromosomes, which made me more patient, caring, accommodative, compassionate, and above all, always helping my kids in the same type of loving environment. Darwin's theory was proven right once again. This very flow of genetic traits from parents to siblings is actually what we inherit. Stories are already written on the genes. Time unfolds the mysteries in the genes slowly. It is just a matter of random reassortment, which we finally receive and display phenotypically. Of course, my first Mother's mother was also an extremely caring, loving, and super accommodative woman. She must have very religiously and with great sincerity gifted her good genes to my first Mother, who handed over the same set of precious gem genes to me. I carry patience, humility, and flexibility as a chromosomal gift from her.

Tolerance was her best asset. She would hardly ever frown. Of course, a few remarks here and there would come as a sudden surprise to all of us. I imbibed this trait of her and always won hearts. Patience and flexibility were other good things of hers. She would never ever come down heavily on any issue but instead would take her time, reassess the situation and finally reset her mindset to make an adjustable move so that everyone feels comfortable. Sarcasm was perhaps unknown to her.

To quote an example of her love for me, she refused to accompany my father to New Delhi when he was to be awarded the prestigious National Award by the then President of India, Giani Zail Singh, in 1985. Being nominated for the countries highest award is always a dream come true for any teacher and their family. I was too young to understand the magnanimity of the award, but my biological mother was very well aware of the importance of the National Award in any teacher's life. Still, she preferred to stay with me happily. Even though I lived in a joint family with my cousins and had my aunts to look after me, she missed my father's prestigious function and preferred to look after me and provide all the necessary supportive stuff as I had to take some vital tests at school. Not only this, she would even miss important family functions if I ever needed her presence by my side. These sacrifices went on without saying. When I feel the same for my kids and try to adjust my hospital timings for their sake, I sometimes feel that I have possessed a dominant "adjustment gene" that controls me accordingly. She was always ready for any level of sacrifice for kids and the family. Learning by following the role models has no substitution. She always stood like Himalaya to support me, so much so that when she got fracture on her wrist bone of right hand, she still would cook food for the entire family with her left hand with the same zeal, enthusiasm, love, motivation and speed. I still remember her favourite words, which she often used to say, "Life has to go on......" The show must go on.

Readers would be surprised and shocked to know that I never addressed my first Mother, my biological mother as Mama or Mummy, but always called her "Aunty." Aunty????? Yes. You got it right. Shocking!!!! Just imagine the profound open-mindedness and a big heart in accepting this and moving forward without grumbling and getting annoyed. To explain things briefly, I grew up in a joint family where I used to address my cousins' mother as mummy. Everyone called my mother aunty and carried the same words and family culture forward without understanding the deep meanings of the words. I knew I was hurting her somewhere but could not rectify myself as there was hardly any objection from her. Truly understanding women, indeed. We can very well understand the generosity of the situation and the amount of retaliation she projected—almost nothing. I did address her "Mamma" in-between at times but could not make it a habit, probably because destiny had some more mothers in store for me in the near future.She was a professional English teacher working in Government Senior Secondary High School, Amritsar, teaching English to higher classes. She loved teaching, and I am pretty sure that she must be the most famous and the most wanted teacher of her time. Her place of work was just within walking distance from our house. She was an early riser, used to take a bath quickly, dress up, and would complete the household chores very happily in the morning. She would then rush to school on foot accompanied by her colleague who lived close by. In fact, she enjoyed doing her work, never grumbled, never frowned. She was indeed very clear in her mind regarding priorities and time tags. She would organise her household chores mixed with her professional responsibilities very nicely and clearly demarcated her primary, secondary and tertiary issues. I learnt to rise early and move early from her. To everyone's surprise, I used to be the first student to reach school. I, too, lived happily without grumbling, without complaining, without hesitating, without much questioning, and without hurting anyone else. Her habits, qualities, characters, methods, values, and morals were deeply admixed with my inner soul that I became a perfect phenotype of hers.

Reading books, newspapers, magazines, reader's digest were her favourite part-time activities. Wren and Martin was her favourite book which I hardly understood. This hobby of hers has been dug deep down in me. She didn't possess good handwriting, which I never liked. Her notes and writings were full of solid substance but not legible. I am sorry to say that I was quite allergic to this part of hers. In sharp contrast, I am bestowed with wonderful handwriting, which I fully attribute to as aGift from my father. He used to write fluently and beautifully as if he were taking a cursive competition. I am quite dogmatic regarding handwriting issues and fully endorse and believe that a man is known by his handwriting. Yes, I do lose my temper with my kids over handwriting part of theirs.

I learned from her the ways to raise kids, to love kids, to understand kids, to stand by them, to be with them, help them, satisfy them, and live a happy, joyous, satisfying life with them in an extremely lovable environment. An environment without an iota of bullying, screaming, shouting, and being annoyed to children. The *beating* was a word that was unheard of. It was only love, love and only love which was available in abundance all the time.

I do thank God for giving me such a nice, caring and lovable biological mother who made my childhood a dream come true. We both just passed time happily, merrily, joyfully.....Time passed on....I entered my school where I encountered my second mother...

Thanks Mama.. Thanks Aunty...

# III
# My Second Mother...

**MY SCHOOLS**
**ST FRANCIS SCHOOL AMRITSAR**
**KHALSA COLLEGE AMRITSAR**
**GOVT MEDICAL COLLEGE AMRITSAR**
**AIIMS NEW DELHI**

First of all, I would like to stand up and bow my head with the deepest respect and utmost regard for the above academic institutions. I have tremendous memories attached to the above institutions but would funnel down my discussion to their role as my second mother in my life.

My first mother raised me and handed me to my second mother to educate me. Yes...every mother does but rarely do we appreciate their roles in our lives. In the mornings, I used to spend my time in the house of my second mother....."The School"..yes....."The St. Francis School, Amritsar."

When I was there, I used to experience a strange but extremely comfortable feeling of belongingness. A feeling of complete satisfaction, a feeling of solace, a feeling of jubilation and a feeling of total contentment enveloped me during my years spent in my school. Revisiting my school in the evenings was the most pleasurable moment of my life, and I used to feel as if my mother was calling me, again and again, to come in her lap to play and grow. Such was the deep connection between me and my primary school from where I passed out carrying a pass certificate of Indian Certificate of Secondary Education (ICSE) for 10 th standard securing decent 87.4 %.

As collective students of St Francis School, we were never ever forced, never ever pressurised, never ever threatened and never ever trained to attain academic perfection only. In fact, the holistic environment of St Francis and its teachers speaks volumes of its motherly role in my development. Our English teachers would definitely stick to our school curriculum but would always go beyond that to make us understand the very meaning of the subject "English." Kishore Sir would make us read newspapers, English novels, the famous Readers Digest, English magazines and would also ensure that we watch good English movies occasionally. His habit of cycling to school was par excellence and adorable. I, many times, thought of myself as Sir Kishore while cycling to school and would imitate his style of English innumerable times while cycling. Mrs Alma, my other English teacher, was beyond human imagination. She would make us sit down silently and always force us joyfully to just write out something on any given topic on a piece of paper in English. She was the one who actually made me learn the art of writing. The initial fear factor....the initial stumble block....the initial trouble of writing was very tactfully handled by her. For the beginners, she would never ever find faults in the handwriting part, grammar part.....but would doubly ensure to acknowledge and pat the student in question so as to build his self-esteem and self-confidence. Since I pursued Cancer Medicine, I hardly got a chance to improve my English, so whatever I read, write, or speak is purely attributed to these two teachers who were par excellent in English.

My Physics teacher, Sir VK Sally, was another gem. Teaching this rough and tough subject artfully, thoughtfully and making us understand all the nitty-gritty of Physics so simply, so logically, so rationally, so humbly and so very happy was his most appreciated skill. He was so very talented that he penned down a book on Physics published by Selina publishers for school students. This book was recommended in almost all schools. Not only this, I made my children realise that the book they study is the one whose author was my Physics teacher in school. Such a fantastic feeling is worth billion dollars. I even took my daughter, Hunar Mahal, to his residence at Rani ka Bagh Amritsar and got the photographs clicked with Sally Sir. I was overjoyed and felt satisfied with doing this and believed that time and again, destiny would make me meet my mothers again and again. All I got from St Francis School, my second mother, was not teachers but happy teachers who happily taught me, happily stood by me, happily bucked me, happily polished and happily refined me.

My chemistry teacher, Sir Puri, had a typical french cut beard. He used to teach chemistry in a way that we, as students, could mix chemistry, feel chemistry and experiment with chemistry in our day to day activities.

This created a powerful impact on my mind. I used to mentally scan, mentally allocate, reorganise and mentally frame the chemical structures of almost all of the things I could see around me in my surroundings. In a way, I was able to see chemistry all around. I could see lactic acid in curd. I could see malic acid in apples. I could see acetic acid in lemons; I could feel the burning sensation of formic acid in a wasp sting, I could feel base and alkalis in soaps, I could feel the salt in table salt, I could see complex chemical structures of paracetamol tablets, and so on....and so on...

He would beautifully write chemical equations on the blackboard, which further fascinated me a lot. Full attendance in chemistry laboratory was automatically ensured keeping in mind the way he would very eloquently and very happily teach us the ABC....of Laboratory chemistry showing us the basic chemistry apparatus right from the beaker, the test tubes, the prongs, the burners, the racks, the pippetes, the micro pipettes, the acids, the alkalis, and would make us ask any question whatsoever would come in our minds and would answer all the queries to our fullest satisfaction and that too very joyfully. Not only this, he would himself take a chemical compound called lead nitrate and heat it in a glass test tube and would ask all of us to record the magical observations. We all would be spellbound to see the typical characteristic crackling sound of lead nitrate on heating, leaving a yellow residue of lead oxide behind and very elegantly emitting a brownish gas called nitrogen dioxide, which would start coming out of the test tube. I would just be wonder struck to see all this and many, many more experiments. Slowly and slowly, I started getting closer and closer to the subject and, in a way, always used to eagerly wait for our chemistry laboratory period with a strange quest.

Laboratory work never haunted me. A strange love affair developed between me and the wonderful world of chemistry. All this got possible because of the uniqueness of Puri Sir's teachings mixed with his magical powers, which enthralled me very badly. All this helped me happily complete my laboratory thesis work during my post-graduation and my DM course. I learnt the art of playing with chemical compounds, experimenting in the chemistry lab and above all, doing things happily in a way that every failure in laboratory work is actually new learning that might open another cascade of chemical reactions perhaps unknown to Mankind. Such strong ionic bonds that developed between me and the Chemistry lab was purely the result of the happy teachings of Puri Sir. Thanks Sir....

My Mathematics teacher, Sir Durga Das, was another powerful personality in my life.

He not only taught mathematics but taught me how to doubt, how to analyse situations, how to critically evaluate problems, how to solve questions in multiple ways and above all, would be glad when I would make mistakes. To err is humans was his favourite saying. He always insisted upon me to make mistakes repeatedly and then move forward with a good amount of learning from each mistake. Under his wings, Mathematics was more of playing a game rather than a subject. To everyone's surprise, my father, too, was a great Mathematics teacher but was more traditional and would never expose me to the wonderful world of endless ways of problem-solving skills. Yes, I did learn the art of good handwriting and the art of drawing neat geometrical figures from him, but I owe my love for Mathematics to Sir Durga Das.

My Biology teacher, Mrs Uppal, was another angel in my life. She was a terrific, very clear, very dogmatic, very assertive and very authoritative biology teacher. Even today, when I meet her, my head automatically bows down with utmost respect and say Good Morning Mam.....!!! She very well knew the art of handling school boys at this very sensitive stage of teaching. The seed for my interest in Human Biology was in fact, first sown by her, which made my vision clearer to choose and pursue Medicine as a career. Thanks Mam, for teaching me biology, especially the chapter on "The Cell." I still remember her each word. I hope she remembers me addressing her son as "Protoplasm"...Thanks, Mam.

Apart from educating me, my second mother, St Francis School, exposed me to "The Mother Nature" as the next beautiful gift with whom I got emotionally connected during my stay at school. My second mother was responsible for making my deep connection with nature. This gift of hers had a far-reaching consequence and a lasting impression on my mind. Even today, I deliberately visit parks near my house, even in the hot summer afternoon, sit down, just to get the same feel of the "School Effect" and to get a silent pat by my second Mother and to silently get associated with "her." The school corridor which led to the senior block of my school was like a royal path surrounded by tall red mulberry trees with their lovely red flowers shed on the ground giving a royal feel of red carpet....was beyond description. It was a warm, beautiful, wonderful, unimaginable and lovely welcome extended by the mother nature of my school to all children.

The Competitive environment, the mad rat race for positions, grades, the winners, the losers, the stage shows, the stage hostings, the game spirits, the cricket matches, the hootings, the shoutings, the clappings at sixes fours, the run-outs, the bolds.....hosting of school functions, enjoying captaincy of school houses, school politics, school elections, school prefects, conspiracies, gossipings, friendships, tussles, and school trips were few another things at which I got sharpened during my stay with my second mother. Life was actually infused each and every second in me during my stay with her. Each day, each sunrise, each sunset, each experience,each interaction, each class, each lecture..... polished me into being a street smart, educated school boy full of manners on the background of love.

Stammering was one of my most disturbing problems, which I faced very bravely. Yes, my schoolmates laughed at me, made fun of me, cut jokes of me, ridiculed me, and simulated me, but the abundance of confidence and lots of positivity with which I was made did not let loose my self-confidence and self-esteem. I always stood strong amongst all the humiliations like a huge mountain. I tried and tried hard to figure out the solutions and ways to resolve my stammering but couldn't really solve it until the day when I was figured out by my English teacher, Kishore Sir, to address the school assembly and speak on "Amritsar Welcomes Lady Diana" for a minute or so. I was to address a gathering of about hundreds of students the very next day and that too in a crispy way so as to wrap up the whole welcome speech in a short span of time. It was a challenge for me. I went home, analysed, prepared and then finalised my short speech for the next morning. Gathering confidence in my mindset, gathering confidence in my walking style, gathering confidence in my overall impression and expressions, I moved forward with little tachycardia, but, surprisingly, my speech went very well, followed by a huge clapping from my school friends. All were wonderstruck and amazed by my fluent speech full of good English words, idioms, witty remarks....Yes, that was the turning point in my stammering. It was purely the self-confidence, self-control, self composition and self positivity with which I was filled up to the brim due to the abundance of love by my many mothers that helped me conquer my problem. As days passed, my stammering improved, and my confidence boosted like anything. From that day onwards, The Sun, The Moon, The Stars, the Universe, the environment, the surroundings, the relations, the relationships, the moments all looked new, refreshed, full of life, vibrant.....I found a new Navdeep in myself....that Navdeep who had won the unimaginable, the tedious and the toughest of the tasks.....Yes....Beating Stammering...

From there onwards, I was ready to take up any challenge in life. I have no words to express my deepest gratitude to my second mother, who helped me overcome my long-standing stammering issue and gave me the meaning of a new life.....I thank St Francis School, right from the core of my heart, for making me more and more confident, grounded and helping me iron out my problems very tactfully.

Schools, school teachers, school environment and the school culture play a very significant role in the making and shaping of an individual both academically and mentally. There is absolutely no substitution for classroom teaching, classroom learning, classroom manners, classroom polishing, classroom brushing, classroom habits, classroom jokes, peer group interactions and peer group emotional entanglements. Schools should always and always be considered as second mothers by each and every student. Schools are an integral part of the personality development journey of any individual. We should and indeed make it a point to thank each one out there whosoever make a difference in the journey of our life. Anyways.....

My second mother, The St Francis School, also gifted me some of my true lifelong best friends with whom I studied, played, laughed and cried for a good ten years but suddenly changed paths once we completed our secondary education. To name a few, Jagmeet Singh Sandhu, Gagandeep Swani, and Vivek were a few good school friends..... Jagmeet was very close and had a deep interest in Mathematics and Physics. He pursued engineering. As expected and to no one's surprise, he got selected in IIT Delhi in 1987. Yes, we did part away in 1987, but the values and the morals which our second Mother taught us kept us spiritually together. No matter we lost in our own worlds to grow in our respective fields and talked to each other only after a pretty long thirty years period and no matter how long we stayed apart, but we still share the same bonding, the same feeling and discuss the same mother, the same school, the same class rooms, the same blackboard, the same coloured chalks, the same teachers, the same examination halls, the same school office, the same Principal, the same school bell, the same church bell, the same benches, the same railings, the same table tennis table, the same jokes, the same evening rounds of the school, the same canteen, the same Church, the same pond of the school, the same late-night Christmas parties of our school, the same....the same..and the same. It was worth billions to be brought up under the shelter of my second Mother....my St Francis School.

Gagandeep is settled in the same city where I reside and practice. Yes, we do meet, but quite infrequently as he is into business. We have totally different paths to track, but yes, his mere presence in Ludhiana makes me feel the very pulse of St Francis School. Vivek is settled in Amritsar. He, too, is into business. Yes, we do meet but very occasionally. Of late, we were closer as I had a chance of treating his mother, who was suffering from Lymphoma. It was indeed a feeling as If I was treating my own mother... I never ever imagined that I would be administering chemotherapy to the mother of my school time friend. We just sat together after a long time, gathered past silently, smiled, and during our eye to eye contact, thousands of memories refreshed in the flick of the wrist. Such strong, intense, deep, long-lasting and emotionally charged relationships with school craft your future so very beautifully that nothing seems impossible to achieve in life. We don't visualise the positive school vibes, but they are so very strong that it ultimately makes an individual into a perfect human being ready to take up any challenge in life. I used to cycle to my second mother's place from my first mother's place. It was such a refreshing experience that I used to feel so very crazy that, at times, I used to cycle fast so as to reach my school early just to hug my second mother. It was a perfect child-mother relationship that created ripples in my heart and soul. I used to lock my bicycle in the cycle stand, hang my bag onto my back and walk over to my class as if the whole school...yes my mother...purely and solely belonged to me, and no one could tear this bond. I would always feel more and more satisfied in school than at my first mother's place...

As days passed in my school, I was sharpened like a perfect arrow to hit and succeed in any sphere of life. Such was the magnanimous effect of my second Mother on me. My school was a perfect second home to me as I was nurtured, educated and made ready to move forward in life. It not only taught me books but also taught me the power to think, the power to question, the power to doubt, the power to take a stand, the power to think out of the box, the power to ponder, the power to take risks, the power to go an extra mile, the power of endurance, the power of perseverance, and taught me millions and trillions of so many small things that it becomes virtually impossible for me to recapitulate and to pen down each and every lesson which my second mother taught me. Not only this, St Francis School taught me to re think, reconsider, redo and revise things, decisions and issues.

It was a fantastic bringing up, perhaps the best in the world.... I have no regrets whatsoever... I still feel that St Francis School provides a holistic platform for the overall development of any child...

In sharp contrast to my home kitchen, my second mother's kitchen, I mean school canteen, was an altogether different world and a different experience. I was exposed to a wide variety of eatables I never ever knew of. Samosas, tikkis, sandwich, tomato rolls, cheese patties, noodles, spring rolls, cold drinks, lemon water, Manchurian, pastries, cream rolls and....and...and what not. The screams, the shoutings, the jostling, the bangings, the pushings, the collisions, the shoulderings.... and.... and... the fun mixed canteen environment was always very inviting. My father made it a point to give me a ten-rupee change to keep in my pocket. He was of the opinion that I should neither be a borrower nor a lender. Yes, I did take eatables from the canteen occasionally, especially the cream rolls, which I still love to eat. I always enjoyed my first mother's home-cooked food, which though monotonous, was good, and I used to relish it a lot. Omelette placed between two chappatis along with mango aachar was a frequent tiffin I carried along from home.

My story about my journey in my school would be incomplete without mentioning the influence of this mother on my faith in God. Yes, exactly. My first biological mother was a partial atheist who visited sacred places very rarely but was of the firm belief that God resided in me and my father and that doing her level best is raising me, and playing the role of an obedient, faithful wife would be enough for her as good deeds.

I don't deny the fact that she was not wrong, as everyone has his own definition, understanding and imagination of God, but in St Francis, I was exposed to a very different God's house, The Church. One good sunny morning when I reached my school around 6.30 AM, I, out of sheer inquisitiveness, entered the Church slowly and steadily. There was complete pin drop silence all around. No one was there. It was a big long hall with so many horizontal benches to sit on. I got afraid but still moved forward, looking at Jesus's Christ's big crucified image hanging exactly on the front wall in front of me. I don't know what happened. I don't know how it happened...I don't know why it happened. I immediately bowed my head in deep respect. I felt as if I had seen and met God. A feeling of completeness enveloped me. My first mother could never have been able to make me understand and experience the Almighty. This very understanding of God and visit to His house was another powerful, spiritual, divine and sacred feel which my first biological mother would never ever have made me feel. I sat there for a few minutes, got internally connected with Him. I started understanding the supreme power of God, started understanding the reason for worshipping important days of God and...and above all, started becoming internally so very grounded that life looked complete in itself. I slowly stepped out of the Church and made it a point to visit it frequently, which I did very religiously and got intimately connected with Him. I used to bow to him silently whenever I used to cross the Church, which happened almost daily. "God lives here" were the three words every student had on his tongue during our stay at St Francis School. This was education beyond imagination. The very feel of The Church, the very feel of its spacious divine hall, the very feel of the holy hymns being recited over there, the very feel of the confession room, the very feel of "The Church father," the very feel of his authoritative personality, the very feel of the lighted candles is so spiritual that I read a lot about Jesus Christ and automatically became a strong and a firm believer that yes, Jesus Christ did visit and stayed in this world, did good things, helped poor, educated the world and showed the path of righteousness.

The confession chamber attracted me the most. Later I found that people come here, accept their wrongdoings, say sorry and experience God's healing through forgiveness. Such was the richness of the teachings in the lap of my second mother, St Francis School. I am truly and deeply indebted to my school for all the good job of refining me during my stay at my second mother's house.

Honestly speaking, I am in tears while writing this part of my life as my experience with this mother is beyond human thinking and imagination. She silently paved my path, silently refined me, silently chiselled me and then finally perfectly fine-tuned me to become a good human being. Schools not only provide education but are the perfect platforms for the overall development of any child. I have never missed my biological mother greater than I have missed my second Mother... "The St Francis School." Not a single day passes when St Francis School is not mentioned, either with my own children or with my own self silently...Such is the power of my second mother.

Leaving back such a beautiful mother who educated me...made me street smart...made me dress like a gentleman daily.....made me wear a tye...made me wear a red blazer for the first time..made me wear a properly ironed out trousers...made me wear school batches... made me class monitor... made me polish my black shoes daily.....made me wear my sports shoes on Fridays.....made my friends.....made me aware of the rise and falls in life...made me ready for the competitive world, made me mad during her absence during prolonged summer and winter vacations...made me wise....made me sit on the railings on the outside...made me expose to canteen world....made my heart skip a beat when our bus got late...was a really really really difficult task....It was indeed excruciating and hurting to say goodbye to my school. Tears literally rolled down my cheeks when I last left my second mother's gate....The school gate. I could hardly walk...my legs suddenly turned into a log of woods......was hard enough to say goodbye to my mother........ Anyhow, I somehow managed to gather my tears and courage. We leave institutions but not memories. So, I moved forward carrying an abundance of love, care and rich memories of St Francis. I many a time dreamt of pursuing my 11th and

12th class from the same school, but somehow couldn't or perhaps couldn't figure out the right way to pursue.

Moving forwards, I got admission to Khalsa College Amritsar, where I completed my Prep and Pre Medical (present-day +1, +2). I had already heard of the great Alumni of Khalsa College Amritsar, including some known personalities like Bishan Singh Bedi, the former captain of the Indian cricket team, Mr Mulk Raj Anand, a famous novelist. Experience in Khalsa College Amritsar was like growing in the lap of another Big academic mother. The richness of its gorgeous, huge, palatial buildings, sprawling lush green grounds mixed with the efforts of the talented teachers helped me in making my first history of my academic career. I topped and stood first in Pre Medical Entrance Test (PMT) conducted by the prestigious Guru Nanak Dev University, Amritsar, in 1987. Not only this, I was bestowed with the award of "The Outstanding Student of the Decade in 1987". Life became unimaginably buoyant.

Suddenly, I was the talk of the town for a few days. My joy knew no bounds, and I was drowning in ecstasy. My photographs got printed in the leading newspapers and magazines of Amritsar and in the Khalsa college bulletin. My neighbours, their families, their extended families, their friends, colleagues, college students, PMT aspirants, even teachers, my mother's colleagues, my father's colleagues all started flocking in my house so as the get a glimpse of the "PMT Topper of 1987" and just to have a talk with me. (Here, I would like the readers to know that it was my 4th Mother who broke this historical news to me telephonically,described in chapter 4.)

These small achievements were actually due to the abundance of love superadded with the lovely, comfortable, joyful and congenial atmosphere given to me by my biological mother during my childhood days combined with the magical teachings of my second mother (Schools). At this point in time, I would like to thank my highly educated teachers of Khalsa College Amritsar, who steered me rightly and inculcated in me the habit of multiple revisions and multiple tests in a session. The secret of every topper is his ability and capability of completing the desired syllabus well ahead of time combined with multiple revisions. Furthermore, I owe my success to Golden Temple's blessings and His benevolence as I was, I am, and I would continue to be a hard core follower of Golden Temple, Amritsar.

My Professors, including my Chemistry Professor Garkhel, my Physics Professor BS Sethi, and my Botany Professor RS Sidhu, played major roles in my success as they were among the senior-most teachers who helped me understand things and clear my unending doubts. My Chemistry teacher, Garkhel Sir, was very fond of Mole Concept and Organic chemistry. He would make me write, rewrite and again re write....many times the value of one mole, two moles, three moles, four moles, five moles, six moles and so on of any chemical compound and that polished me in such a way that chemistry became an integral part of my soul. This teaching style of his, in fact, made me interested in the pharmacology of chemotherapy as anti Cancer drugs were full of complex chemical structures with long IUPAC names. Understanding stereochemistry at this very early age also helped me in my deeper understanding of Molecular Oncology in the future. All this paved my way to attain perfection, which I was aiming at. Thanks Sir, for helping me create history. The result was that one day I became a moving library of knowledge, knowing everything of everything almost anytime, the results of which were very evident when I stood first in the prestigious PMT examination. In fact, I was crafted so very nicely, layer by layer, that nothing seemed impossible for me to achieve in life. Such is the huge impact of love, dignity, respect, and above all, getting a congenial, compassionate and adjustable childhood atmosphere. Childhood relationships and childhood upbringings can either make you or break you...It was indeed impossible for my biological mother to make me a complete person. Yes, she very rightfully handed me over to my second Mother (School) to shape me. Though every mother does the same, it is the way we look at things and acknowledge the right personalities which ultimately help a lot in shaping an individual...The majority of people develop more tunnel vision for their own mothers and disregard all else who play a significant role in shaping their personality. Their Biological Mothers unnecessarily get full credits. It is actually the sum up of all the forces that ultimately guide you, steer you forward, and eventually refine you.

Moving forward, PMT results landed me at Government Medical Amritsar to be trained as a doctor. Being a PMT topper and being declared as the Outstanding Student of the Decade, I was on the mega-hit list for being ragged, which was quite rampant during our old times. Handling people around was a skill that I had already learned from my School days and from the great teachers who shaped and reshaped me. My seniors would daily catch me for humiliation and ragging near the Principal office and near the Pharmacology department, but I successfully turned it to my advantage as my second mother (St Francis School,) whom I had bid goodbye after completing ICSE, had trained me enough to fight all ups and downs of life.

I did my graduation (MBBS) and my post-graduation (MD) in Internal Medicine from this very college. My second mother, Medical College Amritsar, exposed me to a plethora of funny experiences like mass bunking, mass strikes, hootings, raggings, whistlings, shoutings, professional college life, foot clappings, college trips, love affairs, breakups, infatuations, music, dance, annual functions, college sports days, and..and...what not...

As always, I was hungry for positions, medals, grades.... I very well knew the ways to top, the ways to shine, the ways to beat the heat of examinations, the ways to succeed, the ways to rise, the ways to lead. All this helped me stand second in my first professional MBBS examination, putting my foot down heavily and solidly in Medical College. I also earned a distinction in one of the toughest subjects of the first year MBBS course, Anatomy. This, too, set me a class apart from others. Almost all the teachers of Medical College Amritsar started raising eyebrows as distinction in Anatomy was quite unheard of during those days, and getting one was considered the toughest job. Moving forward, my journey was more of a cakewalk as first impressions in professional college meant a lot. I quickly became interested in Cancer Medicine during my second-year MBBS course when I was studying Anti Cancer drugs in Pharmacology. Busulphan, Cyclophosphamide, Nitrogen Mustard and Methotrexate were my most loved and studied drugs. I would read the chapter on Anti Cancer drugs again and again to explore something new every time. I would read in between lines regarding the chemotherapy drugs so much so that unending doubts started surfacing, which

I got cleared during my DM course at AIIMS. Goodman Gillman was our pharmacology Bible which I liked so very much that I still retain my original copy of it in my library at my home in Ludhiana.

In 1993, I got selected as a post graduate student in Internal Medicine. My joy knew no bounds as God granted me three more years to grow and mature in the lap of my second mother. Again being among the top 10 students in the MD entrance examination, I was happily alloted the first Unit, the most wanted Unit Of Medicine department of Guru Nanak Dev Hospital Amritsar, to pursue my post-graduation (MD) in Internal Medicine. Here, I learnt the art of clinical Medicine, the art of history taking, the art of examining every human system systematically, the art of examining sick patients, the art of thinking on a broader basis to diagnose a disease, the art of narrowing down my endless possibilities, the art of performing endless clinical procedures, the art of reading an electrocardiogram, the art of reading electroencephalogram, the art of prescribing medicines, the art of handling emergency medical patients, the art of presenting cases, the art of writing papers and publications, the art of.....the art of...a list which would never ever end perhaps.

While pursuing my MD, I was also exposed to the concept of total commitment towards patients. I got so very busy from this point onwards that Holidays, Sunday's, family functions, family affairs, holidaying, trips, free times, relaxation time.....all got a back seat and were scrapped off from my mind permanently. Only patients, duties, Ward work, studying Medicine, case presentations were my top priorities apart from my own love affair, which too was at its topmost rollercoaster ride.

My second mother not only made me a post-graduate doctor but also gave me my Cancerian love and soul mate of my life, my wife, whom I first met when I was a post-graduate student, and she was in the final year of her graduation. Our first interaction started when I used to take evening classes of final year MBBS students, and she would attend all my classes very religiously, never missing even a single class. And with the passage of time, our student-teacher relationship changed into a complicated emotional entanglement full of ups and downs. All said and done, by the end of 1996, I successfully passed my MD in Internal Medicine and was now fully polished to start my career as a well qualified Medical Specialist and as a physician par excellence.

So, finally in November 1996, my second mother (Medical College Amritsar) said goodbye to me, but during my whole tenure of graduation and post-graduation at Amritsar, an unseen mother used to call me, not very clear in my imagination,which I finally realised that it was my selection at India's top Most Medical School AIIMS New Delhi as post-doctoral DM student in Medical Oncology (Cancer Chemotherapy). Getting a seat in DM Medical Oncology at AIIMS was another milestone achieved. There was just one seat at AIIMS every year, and a whole lot of Medical students had an eye on it. There was a neck to neck competition but due to the abundance of knowledge gained during my stay at Government Medical College, Amritsar, helped me crack my DM entrance examination in the first attempt and that too very joyfully. Doing DM in Cancer Chemotherapy was my dream which came true in July 2004. The journey of my academic career, which started from small St Francis School, Amritsar, ended in AIIMS New Delhi. I was a new, raw and naive doctor from the small city of Amritsar who landed in the lap of my last academic mother, AIIMS New Delhi.

When I was going through the rigours and chills of my DM Course with great dedication, I was constantly attracted to the unseen magnetic power of AIIMS. A strange love developed between the two of us, which deepened gradually with every passage of time. This mother opened my eyes and ear to the world of the Internet, which I had never ever used earlier. Internet, web browsing, emails, google, yahoo, online journals, online teachings, online videos, YouTube, all this was unheard of before I entered AIIMS. With the help of this high technology software, life became easier, more refined, more sophisticated, more connected, more empowered, more interesting, more knowledgeable, more intense and more gripping. I could catch hold of any medical journal anytime, just in the blink of an eye. I, right from my childhood, was more inclined towards academics, always trying to learn more and more, going deeper and deeper, understanding better and better, exploring the new, venturing the unventured and above all was an avid reader of latest medical literature. All this was possible because of the wonderful gift from AIIMS.... "The World of Internet." Blessings from my AIIMS mother were uncountable. She also provided me twenty-four hour access to one of the best libraries of Medical literature. It was full of Medical books, journals, and other necessary ingredients to support and help educate a Medical student. Not only this, I met six powerful personalities during my training at AIIMS who finally cast me into a Cancer doctor and further infused in me the values of Mankind.

First was my Godfather, Prof Dr Vinod Raina, who was instrumental in my selection into the DM course. His Excellency not only taught me Breast Cancer with great dedication but also proved to be my Godfather as he turned down my resignation twice. Strangely due to my father's sickness, I was forced to resign twice from my DM course at AIIMS, but it was only due to his benevolence that I was able to make both ends meet and complete my DM course. Prof Dr Raina was the only person who kept our knowledge of Internal Medicine refreshed as he very frequently interconnected Internal Medical, Medical Oncology and haematology-oncology. Actually, he was exactly right on his part as forgetting basic principles of Internal Medicine while treating Cancer patients is a big blunder and ends up in a disaster. Not only this, he would immediately order for the biopsies of all relevant tissues in case of unexpected deaths of Cancer patients undergoing chemotherapy so as to get deeper insights into the probable cause of unexplained deaths of the patients in question. This definitely improved my insight, expanded my knowledge, provoked me to ponder more and more and ultimately helped Cancer patients to a greater extent. He was the only faculty of Medical Oncology who would forcibly close the Cancer Ward of IRCH to get it cleaned and fumigated so as to cut the incidence of fungal and bacterial infections as low as possible. I would personally call him the guardian of Cancer patients as he can treat Cancer patients in totality. Getting blood sugars tested frequently while on steroids, getting doses of chemotherapy drugs adjusted as per patients performance status, getting doses of vincristine adjusted in older patients, getting voriconazole started right from the earliest suspicion of fungal sepsis, getting exact doses of antibiotics started getting cultures done, getting three ways changed regularly, getting serum Galactomannan test done frequently were some of his favourite life-saving tips and tricks. Such a magnificent mentor, dashing, and powerful personality is hard to find and work with. Working under him, learning from his ocean of experience and wisdom is a dream come true for any doctor aiming to learn Cancer Medicine. We, as residents, occasionally used to call him the tallest leader of the IRCH Medical Oncology department. Prof Dr Raina's technique of harvesting stem cells and then storing stem cells in ordinary refrigeration at four degrees Celsius for four days for autologous stem cell transplant for Myeloma patients proved to be very successful. This very technique of his was totally different from the already established protocols for stem cell transplants. He was class apart for this and proved his point scientifically, for which he received an applaud on a wider platform across the Medical Oncology fraternity.

I have no words whatsoever to extend my gratitude for all the good he has done for me. Thanks so very much Sir.....for keeping me under your wings and making an Amritsar doctor with a rural background into a polished, smart, and evidence-based Medical Oncologist.

The second was Prof Dr Mrs Vinod Kochupillai, who was the Head of Medical Oncology AIIMS at that time. A perfectly genius lady doctor who taught me holistic ways of treating cancer patients. Due to her vast experience in tackling Cancer patients and that too relapsed, refractory and difficult to treat Cancers, she would always think out of the box to work on new innovative ways and methods to combat Cancer. Accepting failures, accepting relapses, accepting deaths, accepting the Nihilistic approach was never her cup of tea. She accepted Cancer as a rough and tough disease but would make me and other residents more rough and tough to handle Cancer. Her logical yet straightforward ways to increase Natural killer Cells (NK Cells) to beat Cancer was a smart strategy that definitely brought her laurels, and I am sure that the Nobel prize is not far away. Taking out a few minutes a day to exercise the way she preached helped lots of Cancer patients.

The third personality who influenced me during my stay at AIIMS was Prof Dr Lalit Kumar. All said and done, I have fallen short of words to express my feelings and love for the multifaceted personality of Dr Lalit. A perfectly woven human being, showing extreme love, care, compassion, dedication, commitment, zeal and enthusiasm. His first house is AIIMS, his first family is Cancer patients, his first breakfast is the morning class at first floor IRCH lecture hall, his first love is the charity for Cancer patients, his first charity is to donate blood and platelets to Cancer patients, his first donation is to arrange free antibiotics, free chemotherapy drugs to poor patients, his first job is to himself put Hickman catheter for transplant patients, his first relaxation is the ward rounds, his first part-time rest is the famous Saturday rounds at second floor IRCH Medical Oncology department, his first...his first...his first...and the list goes on endlessly. He is the life and the most vibrant personality of Medical Oncology. His legacy would continue blessing IRCH in times to come. Sticking to basics, sticking to detailed history taking, sticking to detailed clinical examination, sticking to neat figures, sticking to neat notes, making summaries making perfect discharge cards, attending Oncopathology meets, attending Oncoradiology meets, attending Medical

Oncology grand rounds, listening to residents, their problems, listening to patients, their problems...... all would be taken care of by Dr Lalit in such a way that you would find him totally afresh even in the late evenings. Thanks Sir....Thanks so very much....

The fourth person who influenced me was Prof Dr Atul Sharma, who was the first DM student of the AIIMS Medical Oncology department. He studied at IRCH and then further got appointed as an Assistant professor in IRCH to serve Cancer patients. Apart from being a perfect teacher for Gastrointestinal Cancers, he was very cheerful and jolly, very accommodating and adjusting and above all, always used to be a bridge between all of us as residents and the top faculty. I learnt the art of dressing, the art of wearing perfectly ironed clothes, the art of keeping one's shoes polished even at the busiest hour of the day from Atul Sir. Not only this, his evening clinics for treating Head Neck Cancers at AIIMS were par excellent. I would hardly ever revise my complicated TNM staging for Head Neck Cancer again as he would make us learn the staging on the patients themselves. Such perfect bedside teachings still exist at AIIMS.

The fifth person who further crafted me at AIIMS was Professor Dr Sameer Bakhshi. Prof Sameer is a Senior Pediatric Medical Oncologist at IRCH AIIMS who is very meticulous, very organised, very clear and above all a very helpful personality. I have learned the art of treating kids suffering from Cancer from Prof Sameer. The way he treats, the way he counsels the parents, the way he arranges funds, the way he manages the whole show is really appreciable. AIIMS Cancer Pediatric Unit is like a fish market deluged with Cancer kids, crying parents, nervous attendants , relatives, doctors, paramedics I feel so very privileged to have spent and learnt so much from Sameer Sir that even today, during my own practice, if I am in a fix over some decision, I immediately WhatsApp Sameer Sir and get a quick reply within minutes. Such personalities who keep on helping even when I am no longer a part of AIIMS, speak volumes of their love for Cancer patients and Mankind at large.

Thanks Sir...

Sixth person who finally made me a complete Medical Oncologist was the Molecular Oncology Laboratory of AIIMS. Since I was already interested in Laboratory work right from my school days, I got fascinated by it very soon. A perfect laboratory with lots and lot to learn, lots and lots to do, lots and lots of innovation, lots and lots of new things....this place exposed me to the world of electrophoresis, the world of polymerase chain reactions, extractions of RNA, FISH techniques, quantifications of messenger RNA transcripts, cytogenetics, bone marrow culture, metaphases, stem cell harvesting, stem cell storage, stem cell culture, stem cell viabilities, mononuclear count, and....and. I just miss it day and night...

AIIMS taught me, educated me and helped me earn my decent livelihood. Importance of baseline clinical examination of Cancer patients, baseline history, baseline radiology, baseline PET scans, baseline histopathology, baseline analysis of tumour mutational panel on blocks by Immunohistochemistry, baseline Cytogenetics, baseline quantifications of PCR, was taught to me well and deeply that it has become a habit to keep the baseline record of each and every patient very meticulously. Monitoring the response to chemotherapy too was an integral part of the teaching. Recording observations, drawing neat figures, attaching references, keeping IRCH files neat and clean was another teaching from AIIMS which further refined me. Prof Dr Vinod used to call the Medical record section of the Medical Oncology Unit a Gold Mine of knowledge. He would very frequently assign residents to go to the gold mine, do a retrospective study spanning over twenty years, take out files, interrogate them, and record relevant observations, put them on excel sheet of the computer, go to the statistics department of AIIMS, wrack their head day and night and then finally present the data to bring out something new to learn which ultimately would help Cancer patients and Mankind at large.

Not only this, AIIMS brought me further laurels and helped in creating another history of my academic career as I was the only doctor in the History of Amritsar to do DM in Cancer Chemotherapy from India's top most hospital AIIMS, New Delhi. Not only this, I was the first doctor in the history of Government Medical College Amritsar who did DM from AIIMS New Delhi. Such mothers who bring you name, fame and help open a plethora of endless possibilities in your career are beyond human imagination.

Blessings of my mother didn't end here; AIIMS gave me my lovely Cancerian son, who was born on 3 rd July 2006 at AIIMS. I moved out of AIIMS in July 2007, carrying India's highest degree for treating Cancer patients and a beautiful one-year-old Cancerian Son. Again, leaving AIIMS was another big heartbreak for me, but I got adjusted soon as all my mothers had matured me enough to handle goodbyes.

Briefly, my journey from St Francis School Amritsar to AIIMS New Delhi was like a second mother to me who shaped, reshaped and finally polished me several times, made me go through hundreds and thousands of rollercoaster rides and ultimately made me a good Cancer Doctor who could earn his livelihood, treat Cancer patients and help Mankind at large.

Thanks Mama...

Thanks St Francis School Amritsar, Khalsa College Amritsar

Thanks Govt Medical College, AIIMS New Delhi

Truly indebted to all the above for lifelong...

# IV
# My Third Mother...

## MY MAMI JI

## MRS MANJEET DHILLON

When I was in 2$^{nd}$ class, my Mama Ji (my biological Mothers brother) got married. Of course, I attended the marriage without ever knowing what it was all about, never knowing the real meaning and sense of it but simply enjoyed the village food, the village band, the village drums, the village bhangras, the village music and of course the village sweets, jalebis, laddoos, barfis, ice creams and lots of other sweet dishes. I never thought what that marriage or colourful function or enjoyable gathering had in store for me,another Mother !!!!

The very next day of marriage, I was made to sit in the lap of an unknown lady called Mami ji.....I being a small kid, used to shy a lot and didn't utter a word. But was quite very surprised regarding the new entrant in our family.

As days passed by, my Mama ji and Mami ji got shifted from their village to a place near my house in Amritsar, and that was the turning event in my life. Both of them now used to live relatively close to our house, and our family interaction increased. During this, my Mami ji used to love me, be funny with me, play with me, make lots of mouthwatering dishes for me, celebrate my birthdays with great pomp and show, help me with my homework, do cycling with me, sing and dance with me, narrate lots of stories, help me in overcoming my stammering, a problem which I tried to correct myself.... Not only this, she used to make pancakes.... rumcakes.... pastries and a whole lot of all vegetarian and non-vegetarian mouthwatering dishes for me.All this was never a part of my life. It was a different world... different experience... different relationship... different ways... She was the one who exposed me to all kinds of modern delicious foods and a modern environment of extreme childhood pleasure. My biological mother was a simple, straightforward lady who couldn't cook beyond good traditional sabzis, especially Allo matar ki sabzi, egg bhurji, fish and a few more dishes which can be counted very easily. Birthday celebrations were unheard of till my Mami ji celebrated my 9th birthday with great pomp and show. Colourful balloons, the birthday decorations, beautiful birthday cake, loud music, fun-packed games, endless laughter, chilled icy cokes, spicy Chinese food, and above all, the abundance of love came as an utter surprise. It took me days and days to come out of this. My hidden love for her grew further and further. To my sheer surprise, my Mami ji got a job as a primary teacher in my own school, the St Francis School. My joy knew no bounds. I was lucky to have my third Mother at the same place (school) as my second Mothers (School). I felt too happy but was too small to express this joy and an unusual satisfaction.

Within a year or so, she shifted her house to a place called Rani Ka Bagh, which was quite close to my school but far away from my own house. I was a little disturbed but anyhow managed. She was again a tenant there.

Distances didn't subdue our mutual love as she became over sweet and over caring. She was an extremely understandable lady who continued the same with me but in more depths of motherhood.

As time passed,I grew up further and came to understand that she always longed to have her own beautiful house. Yes, she bought land in Ranjeet Avenue, Amritsar, which in those days was a very remote area, densely populated with trees but sparsely populated with human beings. It was thus quite scary to go there. Making a dream come true by constructing a house in such a remote area seemed next to impossible. But, her dedication, commitment, and burning desire to own a house could not stop her from carrying out the project successfully. She was unstoppable. No rains, no winds, no bad weathers, no scorching summer heat, no harsh winter foggy days,...... nothing..... could stop her in making her dream come true of building her "own" beautiful house at Ranjeet Avenue D block. Even today, her home is no less than a five-star apartment. Being iron-willed, being tough, being tenacious, sticking to decisions and setting goals were some of her qualities which I silently learned from her.

I didn't pass through any turmoil period in my childhood. I was always positive and never felt anything bad as I was constantly flooded with lots and lots of love by my many Mothers. Childhood relationships can either make you or break you. Torturous childhood upbringing with ugly relationships, sarcasm, ugly words, and ugly ways can erode you mentally and permanently shatter your confidence. I was fortunate enough to be away from any of the traumatic childhood periods. Slowly and slowly, I used to imagine my Mami ji as one of the closest women to me in my childhood. Though I could not assign any relation, but I silently knew that she was the one who was always there for me in case of any eventuality, "A perfect nest".... can be the only word which I can think of.....

Now, when I turn back and dive into the past, I strongly feel that she played the role of my third Mother, which I couldn't realise while growing under her shelter. Time spent with her was like time spent in heaven. I felt fully secure with her and always looked forward to seeing her...

Thanks Mama...

My Mami ji..

# V
# My Fourth Mother...

## MRS NISHA VERMA

## MY BEST FRIENDS MOTHER

As time passed in school, I got close to Sumit, one of my good friends. We used to visit each others' houses and developed a thick friendship in a concise period. His mother was another angel in my life. She was totally different from all my other mothers. She was an iron lady with a super positive mindset and a great magnetic power to influence people around her. Reading the public's mindset and then dealing with them accordingly was one of her qualities. She learnt this from dealing with thousands of neurological patients and their attendants who flocked to her house daily as Sumit's father was the most learned and most wanted Neurologist of his time. I, too, silently learnt the art of public dealing, problem-solving, matter resolving and pacifying the crowds from her.

I was a little boy of a primary class who got amazed and attracted towards her powerful persona. Not a day passed when I never met her. She, too, started loving me so very much that she used to call me her third son. As Sumit and I grew up together, we were blessed enough to get admission to the same Medical College for pursuing higher studies to be trained as doctors. The Medical College was within walking distance from Sumit's house. His house became a common destination for us. She always called me an academic superstar which was enough to keep my spirits and confidence very high. Such positive words, a positive attitude, positive environment, positive feel, positive world, positive possibilities and positive patting was enough to push me to my limits. Such mothers who aren't your biological mothers but still kick your morale high and whose kids are with you and that too competing with you for the same Medical seat through same competitive examination are beyond description. Such an unbiased attitude, such an encouraging attitude and that too flowing so very naturally, is unheard of even in the worlds greatest histories

She was the one who broke the historical news of my topping in PMT through a phone call and congratulated me so very sweetly and lovingly that her words still echo in my ear whenever I recall my old memories. "Navdeep beta, YOU TOPPED!!!!....You have made me more proud....I am proud of you....Sumit is 8$^{th}$. Come soon...We all will celebrate....." were her loving words. Her voice was loud, clear and full of joy, without an iota of ill-feeling.

Gallons of water has flown under the bridges since we last met, but the amount of silent love and silent respect we share for each other is so mutual that distances, borders, and boundaries are just a matter of words....

Me and Sumit, both were served good rich food.... rich, healthy drinks and above all, I always used to feel Sumit's home as my first home due to the wonderful hospitality extended by her. Unlimited love and unlimited respect were what I used to receive from her. She was a woman with endless possibilities. Stopping and thinking was never a part of her life. Moving forward despite all odds and conquering the unconquered was always her passion. I can hardly narrate an incident when she would feel low or anything could stop her in life. I indeed feel very lucky to have grown under her wings. Her amazing smiling nature, her rich positive body language, perfect aggression, unending positivity......speaks volumes of her personality. She would be ready to help anyone anytime. Simply putting forward, she was a class apart. Even today, when I feel low, I sit down and think about her and gather lots and lots of super amazing energy just by recollecting her in my memories which helps me forget the small nitty-gritty of daily life. I secretly open her super smiling display image of WhatsApp to gain strength. She was a perfect mother with extraordinary qualities....

Thanks Mama...

My Nisha aunty...

# VI
# My Fifth Mother...

## MY MOTHER IN LAW
## DR SAROJ GOYAL

Needless to say, my book would be incomplete without mentioning the influence of my mother in law in my life. This part of writing is obviously going to be one of the most challenging ones considering the most sensitive relationships between both of us.

As would be evident from her name, things need not be explained. Love marriages are hard to digest and accept in Indian traditional culture and the way things jostle around in India. I found my Hindhu Cancerian love in my second Mothers campus (Medical College Amritsar), but translating my emotional and spiritual ties with her into a practical legal family bond was a very, very tough job. My would-be mother in law particularly was a hard nut to crack. She was a staunch and a rigid follower of Hinduism. Marrying her eldest daughter to a Jat Sikh family was hard to digest for her. She was all very confident regarding the reversal of things, but events didn't work in the way she thought and predicted. She tried her level best to persuade her daughter and to reset her mindset but failed miserably. Anyways, after all ups and downs as typically happen in any traditional Hindi Indian romantic film, love won, and we finally got married on 4th August 1996.

"Dilwale Dulhania Le Jayange" got rewritten in 1996. Everyone from my family was quick in getting us legally married as early as possible before my would-be mother in law started frowning again. The day came...yes...my marriage day...I got dressed up nicely wearing sober clothes, a white shirt, black trousers and marron turban, keeping my mouth shut, eyes open, having a vacant stare and a wax-like face. My family was so very happy that my father gifted me a brand new Maruti 800 a week before my marriage. My family members and I started towards the marriage venue on that very car, driving it all by myself....as if I was being planned to be beheaded over there. There, I felt as if I was sitting on a time bomb ready to get exploded anytime during the traditional "pheras" during our marriage ceremony, which was carried out by "Pandit ji" in front of "Agni Devta" in a typical Hindu Marriage style. The environment was so charged that relatives from both sides were attending more of a horror show than a happy Indian marriage despite wonderful hospitality extended in Amritsar's the then best 5-star hotel "The Mohan International" by my in-laws. Even the hoteliers and the waiters over there were caught unaware of this "Silent marriage." I was so very fearful that I hardly made eye to eye contact with my mother-in-law, who must be thinking of me as an alien. During our marriage, the atmosphere was silent, with a little whispering here and a little whispering there. I was being interrogated, analysed and scrutinised from head to toe so meticulously and vigilantly by my in-laws as if I had committed some crime of loving their daughter. The only point of solace were the sweet words "jiju" being spoken by my sister in law, Nonika, who was sitting beside me. "Jiju" words made me settle down, calm down and finally made me reassure of my legal marriage.

Anyways....we settled down. Time passed. We started opening with each other. The emotional deluge started settling. Talks started between my mother in law and me. From monosyllables to few words to few sentences to full-fledged hilarious talks started very shortly. Things settled down soon between us. Soon she realised that yes, I too, was a smart, educated boy for her beautiful daughter. For this, I thank all my mothers who had made me smart enough to handle undulations in life....All said and done, my mother in law is a retired government doctor, a great homemaker and an amazing multitasker. She is at her best in cooking traditional delicious vegetarian homemade food. To my utter surprise, she could cook any Indian dish in the flick of the wrist and keep the guest's mouthwatering for hours. Learning new recipes and experimenting with innovation in cooking is her passion for which she deserves an applaud. My kids always long for her "Panner ki paranthi" and delicious lady finger whenever they visit Nani's place.

Fiddling with clothes is another best part of her. You give her any cloth; she would come up with some beautiful designers dresses which would even surprise the best of the boutique walas. Gardening is another hobby that keeps her busy and engorged. I remember my early days of marriage when I used to visit her place when I would be made to sit among lots of flower pots surrounding me, and the place would give more of a hill stations feel rather a traditional urban house as it was full of thick green vegetation, dense tress and lots of bushes.

She just loves travelling, and that too is an unlimited and unconditional one. We often travelled together. She would always make the entire trip lovely and full of life with her lively hilarious talks and jovial remarks. I still remember my US trip when she accompanied me and made my journey an unforgettable experience. She would not allow anyone to get loose and take rest but would keep on moving from one place to another as if she needed to see and explore each and every niche of the world. She has a tremendous amount of energy and is a constant source of renewable energy all the way along for others..... She dislikes tiredness.

The bargaining power of my mother in law is beyond imagination. She would immediately bring the rates of anything by her sheer skill, which I tried to learn and apply multiple times but failed miserably. This quality of hers made me understand the real worth of things that were being sold in the market at such skyrocketing prices that it is indeed very difficult for an ordinary man to keep both ends meet. But, on a lighter note, her bargaining power failed in human relationships, and she was unable to separate us despite all odds...

Cooking, gardening, clothing, travelling and bargaining were never a cup of my tea, but all this has been taught to me by my 5$^{th}$ mother. My mother in law.

Thanks Mama...

My mother in law...

# VII
# My Sixth Mother...

## MY ELDERLY FEMALE CANCER PATIENTS

I am an Oncologist. More specifically, an Oncologist who treat Cancer patients by chemotherapy. Breast and Ovarian cancers are quite common in the region where I practice. I frequently encounter these patients more often than any other cancer patient. Most of my Breast Cancer patients are beyond 60 years of age and usually address me by the word "Beta," which in English means "Son."

This "Beta" word echoes in my mind both day and night. The soothing effect of this very word makes me rewire myself and makes me think that I am blessed with so many mothers around me each day that I have to give my best to protect motherhood at large. I receive unending blessings, unending love, unending respect and unending trust from all my elderly female Cancer patients whom I treat day and night. They not only discuss their disease but very often open their heart with me. I am an extremely patient listener, silently understanding and learning a lot from their wisdom. Listening patiently is an inherited trait from my biological mother. I know each question and statement need not be answered, so I just listen quietly. The mistake we as humans make is to respond to everyone but should learn from others' experiences. I know, and I very well understand, that I cannot breach patients' privacy, and I need to respect and blindly follow Medical ethical standards. Naming any one female patient would be a gross violation of my ethical domain.

Cancer is such an emotionally devastating disease that I have learned the deeper meaning of "LIFE" from my Cancer patients. Understanding motivation, understanding inner voices, understanding commitments, understanding the real meaning of being positive, understanding time tags, understanding life, understanding death, understanding constant insecurity, understanding emotional turmoils, understanding financial losses, understanding financial insecurities, understanding financial management in tough times, understanding priorities, understanding priorities in tough times, understanding relationships, understanding relationships in touching times, understanding commitments, understanding end of life issues, understanding "Wills," understanding family tags, understanding solace, understanding loneliness, understanding the real deeper hidden meaning of tears is all that I learnt from my elderly female Cancer patients, which further helped me in understanding Mankind at large.

All my female Cancer patients make me learn so much about life, that too so very deeply that it has actually altered my perception towards humanity. I very distinctly remember that evening when one of my dying Breast Cancer patients declared that I had to be present and hold her hand till she slept off finally. Such powerful touchy moments stirred my soul. I, on one side and her eldest son on the other side of the bed, who is a senior practising lawyer at Ludhiana, held her hand and finally bid goodbye to her...

This reminds me of another elderly female Cancer patient. I was stunned to get a call from her and address me as... "Navdeep, do you remember me?" I was your teacher in Government Medical College Amritsar....I am suffering from Ovarian Cancer, and I want to get treated by you."

Yes, she definitely told me her name. I quickly recollected her and was at first shocked to listen to this news but immediately assured her the best possible way in which I could extend my help. She got treated by me, took all chemotherapy sessions from me but unfortunately, due to her advanced disease could not survive beyond a few years. We used to sit together, chat together, eat together, laugh together, and at times, wept together, understood life together, recollected all the old memories of Medical College Amritsar in a more holistic way. She was my patient, who had taught me "Microbiology" during my graduation times and gave me an opportunity to treat her. Such moments and experiences of treating your own teacher are actually phenomenal. The amount of trust she had in me, the amount of confidence she had in me, the amount of faith she had in me made me more and more committed.

Such deep connections, which I develop silently with my elderly Cancer patients, go right into my heart and soul to make me stronger, more attached, more sentimental, more respectful and more committed. Not only this, it also ignites me to read more, study more and keep myself abreast with the latest happenings in the world of cancer treatment so that I am empowered in a more powerful way to help all my patients to get rid of their disease. For this, I frequently brush up my knowledge and try checking the latest guidelines pertaining to each and every Cancer. I make it a point to refresh my Cancer Medicine knowledge every now and then to help humanity at large. For this, I usually stick to well defined and well-established protocols published across the globe. NCCN guidelines are one of my favourite ones to help Cancer patients. (National Comprehensive Cancer Network guidelines). NCCN is a non-profitable alliance of thirty-one leading Cancer Centres in the United States of America devoted to Cancer Care and research. Molecular Oncology is a fast developing branch of Cancer Medicine that has successfully come up with groundbreaking chemotherapies for Cancer patients helping them get rid of their disease in a more targeted and tailored manner. Nihilism has paved the way to optimism. Our goals have been redefined as Molecular Oncology has made us understand the basic drivers of the Cancer in question. Days and days of research in Cancer Medicine has ultimately succeeded in finding a key for almost every Cancer. Not only this, the dreadful side effects of chemotherapy has also been taken care of. Gone are the days of vomiting, gone are the days of prolonged low blood counts, gone are the days of fever and gone are the days of alopecia. Chemotherapy is no longer a horror world.

"You need to see to believe" is an axiom known to me for years but understood only after interacting with thousands and thousands of my Cancer patients. The first-hand experience which they all share is worth million scientific studies. A lot of my Oncology colleagues get surprised when I say that I am poor at publishing data. Majority of my time is spent in counselling, understanding, listening and then answering each and every question of the patient. In fact, my sixth Mother encompasses one to one interaction of mine with thousand and thousand of elderly female Cancer patients.... Not only this, spreading positivity and helping Cancer patients is my first priority rather than playing academic athletics with my own colleagues.

The real meaning of death, the real feel of dying, the real fear of dying, the real trauma of dying, the real meaning of life after death is all that has been more sentimentally, more softly and more clearly taught to me by all my dying Cancer patients....

I just want to share an observation that surfaced and clicked to me when I correlate the timing of the many deaths of my Cancer patients with the entry of some newborns in their families...Some pregnant lady would deliver around the death of the patient in question...in that family...

Is this His way of rebirths?

Is this His way of transfer of souls? Is this pure coincidence?

I think it can be anyone's guess....but it is quite thought-provoking....

Thanks Mama...

Thanks All...

# VIII
# In A Nutshell

## CUTTING A LONG STORY SHORT

My first Mother (my biological mother) brought me into this world, reared and raised me with the abundance of love, took care of me and silently taught me love, intimacy, tenderness, extreme patience, unending humility, flexibility and compassion. Above all, I tried to simulate her in raising my own kids.

Thanks Mama...

My second Mother (My St Francis School Amritsar, Khalsa College Amritsar, Government Medical College Amritsar and AIIMS New Delhi) educated me, helped me develop good habits, refined me to interact with my colleagues, helped me develop my career and finally made me earn my livelihood and made be financially independent. Thanks St Francis, Thanks Khalsa College, Thanks Govt Medical College, Thanks AIIMS.

Thanks Mama...

My third Mother (My Mami ji) infused lots of vibrant life, full of refreshing feelings, lots and lots of newer things to learn and ultimately showed me the importance of essential days in one's life...I could feel the glimpse of Shoba De in her....

Thanks Mama...

My fourth Mother (My friend's Mother) always made me feel on top of the world, always made me feel like a small academic superstar, showering all her praises and positivity on me and made me buoyant all the time. Today, If I am all positive, the whole credit goes to her, and I would always and always be indebted to her for showing me the ways of life....and the methods to move forward despite all odds and to keep all gates open...

Thanks Mama...

My fifth Mother (My Mother in law)brought my love into this world. Despite all apprehensions of mine, she loved and adored me and exposed me to an entirely different beautiful world of cooking, travelling, gardening and, of course, bargaining in my life....

Thanks Mama...

My sixth Mother (My elderly female patients) taught me many experiences, especially relating to the whole gamut and spectrum revolving around end of life issues....uncertainties, and death.

Thanks Mama...

# IX

# Where Are My Six Mothers At Present?

My first Mother (My Biological Mother)

Habits die hard. Obviously, she is with me, still loving me much more than before, still pampering me, still cooking "egg bhurji," "tomato fish," and now a new dish "jeera Aaloo" for me, and now, of course, for my family too. Not only this, she is rewriting history by taking care of my kids in a much more sentimentally emotional world of paradise that I truly hope that my children would come up with the second edition of this book once they grow up...

My second Mother (My Schools)

They, too, are in the same place. I do visit them, though infrequently, but naturally, get highly emotional and touched. They are all with me all the time in my heart, full of life, educating me again and making me shed tears of extreme joy. All of them have grown bigger, much better, more revolutionised and more sophisticated, keeping in view the sea change that has occurred in technology in the last thirty years. They are continuously nurturing more and more kids in their laps and are educating them in a more holistic way to make them way better academically, emotionally, physically and spiritually.

My third Mother (My Mami ji)

She too is the same, more refined, more lively, more jovial and has acquired much more life values.... She stays in the same city as before...about two hours drive from me. I do meet her at times. She is presently engorged with her boutique, gardening, raising grandchildren and taking care of her big house at Ranjeet Avenue and her dog.

My fourth Mother (My Friend's Mother)

She, too, is in the pink of her health, spreading positivity all around in the US and taking care of her grandchildren in a much more refined method...This Mother of mine is hard to forget...Neither her morale would go down, nor she would allow others to dip....I am pretty sure that her extended family in the US must be so very proud of her and must be taking good care of her......Putting simply forward, she is a big big asset to Mankind....

My fifth Mother (My Mother in Law)

She, too, is enjoying life frequently shuttling between India and Phoenix, where my brother in law lives and now has attained perfection in cooking and gardening.....Watching TV serials is her another love which she enjoys to her fullest satisfaction. She is a great homemaker.

My sixth Mother (My Elderly Female Cancer Patients)

They all are good, happy, bolder, stronger, getting more beautiful with the passage of time with their new hair growths post chemotherapies, getting more and more positive and emotionally more powerful as days pass, getting more committed, and are in fact, enjoying life to their fullest possible ways despite all odds "Zindagi na milege dobara" feel....

I myself feel to be extremely privileged to have grown under the umbrella of so many Mothers. I am the sum-up of all the inherited genetic characters from my biological mother mixed with acquired environmental influences of all the rest of the mothers. My habits, my academics, my character, my ways of life, the way I talk, the way I walk, the way I dress up, the way I communicate, the way I interact, the way I organise things, the way I write, the way I speak, the way I lead, the way I compete, the way I love, the way I solve problems, the way I treat, the way I am....yes....the way I am..... the onus goes wholeheartedly to all my 6 Mothers who crafted me layer by layer so very nicely and compassionately to finally make "Navdeep".....an educated well mannered well dressed Cancer Super specialist who values Mankind, motherhood, Womanhood, family, extended families, relations, relationships, patients, colleagues, friends, friendships,...... Yes, I do miss all my mothers. Apart from my biological mother, who lives with me and my mother-in-law, who meets me very frequently, I miss my second Mother the most and that too St Francis School. I don't know why.....

Anyways, sweet, wonderful rich memories are my greatest assets for which I don't need a space, a bank locker, a security guard.....all that I need is a heart. With every beat of my heart, my memories refreshen up like a fountain and spread to each and every niche of my body to rejuvenate my soul and me. I know that all my distant mothers would definitely be remembering me every now and then and feel the same magical effects in them...... Such is the deep, lasting love we share together....

Thank you Mamma...

Love you all...

# X
# What Was Never Taught To Me

Yes, my small bouquet would definitely be incomplete if I don't expose my shortcomings, my incomplete learning lessons....and obviously if I don't mention what was never ever taught to me by my mothers...or else...what were the things which I learnt later on that should have been taught earlier.

Starting from my biological mother, she never taught me sadness, dejections... rejections... depressions... bad times... Well, after getting a plethora of lifetime experiences, I personally do feel that children should definitely be exposed to or at least taught or made well aware of all these difficulties of life by biological mothers because many of us struggle hard while handling such odd situations during our bringing up that ultimately erode us mentally and make us lose our self-confidence and self-control. Children who aren't so strong take these difficulties seriously and have tough times handling them logically and rationally. They are at times forced to take extreme steps. Being mentally, physically and spiritually strong is one of the biggest assets which one can possess and should be taught right from the school days as it takes time to master them. Being street smart is another quality to be possessed in abundance and should definitely be included in the school curriculum.

My second mother, my academic schools educated me but never taught me how to be financially independent, how to look for jobs, how to create jobs, how to be a good entrepreneur, how to draft impressive personal resumes, how to communicate professionally, how to handle top managements of the hospitals, how to handle workplace issues, how to handle workplace stress, how to handle hospital politics, how to handle interpersonal relationships at the hospital, how to handle public, how to handle media, how to handle the press, how to handle seniors, how to handle juniors, how to handle paramedical staff, and above all, how to handle and make a balance between your personal and professional life.

Teaching leadership qualities, teaching personal financial management, teaching multitasking, teaching social networking, teaching being more skilfull...are a must to be taught during our school days....

My third Mother, my Mami ji, never pointed out my mistakes which I guess must have done inadvertently many times during my stay with her. Obviously, she loved me, for which I would be indebted to her life long. Still, I feel that pointing mistakes and then making one understand them logically and realise them go a long way in achieving perfection for anyone.

My fourth Mother, my friend's mother, Nisha aunty, did point out my mistakes but very infrequently. Learning never ends. Yes, I did take them seriously and used to improve upon them. She was indeed a perfect mother who was so very busy in her household chores that I always longed to be with her and spend more time with her. I feel sad that she did not make me aware of the possible avenues that can open gates to opportunities waiting for Indian doctors abroad. She left India around 1993. I have no grudge against her but, at times, I feel so very lonely because living with her, speaking to her, growing under her umbrella was so addictive that it was really very hard for me to forget her. Whenever I pass in front of her palatial house in Amritsar, I get reconnected with her spiritually and get lots of silent love, blessings, and motivation.

My fifth Mother, my mother in law, didn't teach me how to handle a Cancerian wife. Cancerians have strong mood changes and are emotionally labile. Obviously, this part of her daughter was definitely known to her, but due to our constrained relations earlier on, she kept it close to her. Anyways, it was lovely exploring this part of my wife myself.

My sixth Mother

My innumerable female Cancer patients never pointed out my mistakes which I feel is a strong hurdle in attaining perfection as a doctor and in handling human relations and understanding Cancer around.

Anyways...

Thanks to God for giving me 6 mothers...

I thank all my 6 mothers to transform a small boy from a small city of Amritsar, who lived in a small house, in a small street, in a small family, who fought stammering during his childhood into a very well educated, fluently speaking polished Cancer doctor who presently lives in a big city, owns a big house, has a big family, works as a Senior Consultant Medical Oncology and Hematology Oncology in a big hospital, dreams big, thinks big, dares big, take big risks and above all is a big lover of Cancer patients and Mankind at large......

Thank you all...
Thanks Mama...